Humpy the Whale

by Charles Racine
illustrated by Michael LaDuca

Soul'd Out Publishing House

humpythewhale.com

Dedicated to the beauty and magic of the Hawaiian Islands.

Published by Soul'd Out Publishing House

humpythewhale.com

Illustrations by Michael LaDuca

Manufactured in the United States.CPSIA Compliance Information:

Batch # 812

For further information contact RJ Communications, 800-621-2556.

ISBN 978-0-578-09800-5

Humpy the whale was born on New Year's Day. Every whale in Maui was excited because it meant they would have another friend to play with.

Humpy was different because he was born too small. Most whales are born about 10-12 feet long—as big as a car. Humpy was only the size of a bicycle.

Soon, all the other whales started to notice that he wasn't growing at all. Other baby whales started making jokes about him.

The baby whales lined up for breaching practice; that's when whales jump up out of the water and make a huge splash.

Humpy tried and tried but he couldn't get even half way up, because he was too small.

Humpy swam, spouted and shouted, **"I have an idea."**
"I'm going to find new friends to play with," he told his parents.

"Humpy, we will always love you no matter how small you are, just be careful—and come back before we go to Alaska," his parents said.

"Okay, I love you," Humpy said as he slapped his tail on top of the water.

"We love you too," his parents said as they also slapped their tails.

As Humpy swam off, he noticed a school of Hawaiian state fish-humuhumunukunukuapua'a —were playing together. Humpy swam closer,

"Hi, I'm Humpy. What are your names?"

They looked at him, and became frightened.

"Yikes!" They yelled, scattering in all different directions.

Humpy was sad.

Then Humpy noticed some sea turtles playing catch with their starfish friends; Humpy swam up to join in. Timmy the turtle threw the starfish a little far and it landed right next to Humpy, so he picked it up.

"Can I Play?" Humpy asked as he picked up the starfish.

"Maybe. Throw it over here," Timmy the turtle said.

Humpy threw the starfish so far through the water that they couldn't even see it.

"Now look what you've done!" Timmy the turtle said.

"Oops, Sorry!" Humpy felt bad for ruining their game.

"Go find some friends your own size to play with," Timmy the turtle said.

Then Humpy swam near the dolphins and they were surfing in and out of the waves which looked like fun to Humpy.

"Do you mind if I join you?" Humpy was always polite and asked first.

A wave came and Humpy got in everyone's way.

"Hey! What are you doing? You can't surf," Danny the dolphin shouted.

"Can you teach me?" Humpy asked.

"You're too different. Go to the other side of the island; you can learn there," Danny the dolphin laughed.

When Humpy reached the other side of the island he saw a different kind of fish; they were sharks.

"Hi, can I play with you?" Humpy asked the creatures.

"You want to play with us? No one ever plays with us," Toothy the shark said.

"I know how that feels. All the other sea creatures said I was too different to play with them, so I gave up trying," Humpy told him.

"Never give up. Even though we're different we can jump higher, swim faster, and dive deeper than most of the fish in the ocean. It's not about your size, it's about wanting to try the best you can at everything you do, friend," Toothy the shark said.

"Did you call me friend?" Humpy asked.

"Anyone as brave as you who swims around the island, trying new things, is certainly a friend of ours," Toothy the shark replied.

Humpy swam, spouted and shouted, **"I have an idea. Could you teach me how to do those things?"**

"Sure. It's easy to learn when you're having fun," Toothy the shark replied.

Within a few weeks, Humpy was diving deeper, jumping higher and swimming faster than he ever did before. Soon, it was time to go back to his parents.

"Thank you. You are great friends,"
Humpy said as he began his swim back home.

Toothy the shark shouted, **"Goodbye Humpy, thanks for not being scared of us."**

On his way back, he swam past the surfing dolphins again. Humpy swam, spouted and shouted, **"I have an idea."**

A giant wave came and this time Humpy's new speed helped him catch the wave first.

The dolphins were shocked, Humpy was surfing better than they were.

"Wow! He's awesome now. Who taught you?" Danny the dolphin asked.

"My friend Toothy the shark," Humpy said proudly.

"Come back anytime," Danny the dolphin said.

He saw the turtles again, who were all at the edge of a sea cliff looking unhappy.

"What's wrong?" Humpy asked.

"All of our starfish are at the bottom of the sea and it's too deep for us to dive down to get any to play with," Timmy the turtle answered.

Humpy swam, spouted and shouted, **"I have an idea."**

Humpy remembered his shark training and his tail started flapping as he dove deep down the side of the sea cliff. Humpy quickly came back with a starfish in his fin.

"Wow! That was fast," Timmy the turtle thanked Humpy.

"You're welcome," Humpy said as he swam away.

"When you come back you can play with us anytime," Timmy the turtle said.

Humpy returned to his mom and dad.

"Aloha Humpy, did you have a fun adventure?" His parents asked.

"Yes, a great adventure. Have the other whales graduated from school yet?" Humpy asked.

"It's going on now," his parents said.

When he got to graduation he noticed that all the baby whales were full-sized now—about 40 feet long—the size of a school bus. Humpy was still only as big as a dolphin or a shark.

"Hey, look who's back. Looks like he was born yesterday," the student whales laughed.

For their final test the student whales would perform a full breach, spinning almost half way around while in the air.

Humpy swam, spouted and shouted, **"I have an idea."**

Humpy dove down into the ocean; he went so deep that the others could barely see him.

Then, like a rocket, he shot up out of the water doing a full spin and a half. No one had ever done that before. The whales were amazed. The teachers gave him an A+ making his parents proud. The other whales even asked Humpy to teach them how to jump higher.

Now it was time for the whales to head to Alaska, but something was stopping them.

"What's going on?" Humpy asked his parents.

"A group of sharks are blocking our way," they told Humpy.

Before his parents could stop him, Humpy swam over to the sharks.

Toothy the shark recognized him. **"Hi Humpy, how's it going friend?"**

"Great! I had the biggest jump in the whole school," Humpy said proudly.

"We knew you would do well," Toothy the shark replied.

Humpy then said politely, **"All the whales are trying to go this way to Alaska, but they're all scared of you."**

"See, we told you Humpy, they never took the time to get to know us like you did," Toothy the shark said.

"If you can just move over a little so we can pass, I'll be able to show them that you're not so scary after all," Humpy explained.

"That sounds like a good deal Humpy. Visit us when you come back," Toothy the shark said and the sharks swam away.

When Humpy returned, the whales were all shocked and asked, **"How did you do that?"**

"I just talked to them. Just because they look different, doesn't mean they want to be treated differently," Humpy said.

Wally, the oldest whale, swam forward and said, **"Humpy, I am really impressed with your growth, not in size, but in your ability to be friends with other creatures of the sea; I want you to help lead the pack back to Alaska. We can learn a lot from you."**

What a great honor! Humpy became one of the smallest whales with the greatest reputation.

Humpy returned the next year and he kept his promise to visit with all the friends he had met before. He even played a little starfish catch with Timmy the turtle.

Now, when whales are born with anything different about them, no one makes fun of them. Instead they say, **"You're lucky. That's how Humpy became one of the most popular whales around."**

Humpy still comes to Maui each year and visits with his friends and always makes new ones too.